To Live in Autumn

Zeina Hashem Beck

T0339190

To Live in Autumn

POEMS

Zeina Hashem Beck

The Backwaters Press

© 2014 by Zeina Hashem Beck

The Backwaters Press
3502 North 52nd St.
Omaha, NE 68104-3506
402-451-4052

The Backwaters Press

www.thebackwaterspress.org

Published September 2014 by The Backwaters Press
Printed in the United States of America
Cover art by Yazan Halwani
Cover design by Chris Bristol
Interior design and typesetting by Susan Ramundo, SR Desktop Services
The text of this book is set in Adobe Garamond Pro

ISBN 13: 978-1-935218-35-7

First Edition

14 15 16 17 18 5 4 3 2 1

Library of Congress Control Number: 2014945850

For Mom, who knew
For Marwan, who loves
For Leina and Aya, who (I hope) will experience
For Huda, who shared
For my Beirut, who inspires.

"You had such a vision of the street
As the street hardly understands."

—T.S. ELIOT

To Live in Autumn

I. Winged Carrots

II. Portrait of a Woman with a Cigarette

III. The Language of *Salaam*

IV. Palimpsest City

V. Ten Years Later in a Different Bar

To Live in Autumn

Zeina Hashem Beck

I.
Winged
Carrots

A Few Love Lines to Beirut

Memories
age faster than us,
die sooner,
disappear silently like hair,
without a passing date, a suicide note, a last vowel.
And what are we then? What
are we then? Surely
the shadow of a memory,
the memory of a shadow—

I am tired, tired of trying
to balance your name on my breath,
summon your street rhythm in the sway
of my hips, my steps,
recall your storm, your warmth,
on my arms, my legs;
I'm tired of trying
to repeat you in my head.

To Hamra

Every morning Umm Naji
makes a lousy joke
as she stirs our coffee.
We look at her dirty nails,
we hold the warm paper cups,
walk
across streets that are endless
in their endless repetitions,
small labyrinths
we have memorized,
familiar labyrinths
in which we get lost on purpose.

Here is the yellow coffee shop,
and another,
and another,
where our fathers curl politics
with their cigar smoke
all day,
measure poetry
with their sugar spoons
and say,
"The *situation* is bad again,
it is bad again."

Here is Modca,
the ancient coffee shop,
where memories cling to the walls
like a wild vine that sprouts
voices and smoke and small conversations.
Here is Modca,
the ancient coffee shop,
turning into a Vero Moda,
no more spoons or cigarettes or clatter of cups—
history buried in clothes,
outshone by Starbucks.

Here is the small cassette shop
in which the fat man barely fits,
in which the fat man sings and spits,
and nods and nods,
as if to God,
saying business is slower
than old age,
releasing Arabic music
into crowded streets that move
to the inborn beat,
here is the small cassette shop,
and another,
and another.

Here is the flower shop,
and another,
and another.
They all have the same name,
insist they're not the same—
a sidewalk of flowers and dust.
We decide to buy the white lilies,
just because they're flowers,
just because they're white,
just because they're lilies.

Here is the deserted theater
where the bald man sighs
into a red telephone,
shouts at his wife,
cries
his bills, his anger away,
you'd never expect
emotions
inside the smell of old semen
and posters of movies that never really play.
Here is the deserted theater,
and another,
and another.

Here is the whorehouse,
where the fat woman gathers
old age in a chair,
promises cab drivers a good time
with the worn beauties inside,
leaning bare on the bar,
leaning, withering
in the smoke of a cheap cigar,
and another,
and another.

Here is the leftist pub,
where the gray man smiles,
plays the *oud*
(could wood and strings reach the soul like that?)
he sings,
his rough voice sinks
through us like a rock,
Umm Kulthum, Fairuz, Abdel Halim,
ya leil ya ein,
the most famous words in our language,
ya leil ya ein,
we clap and dance and hope
the term papers will write themselves,
here is the leftist pub,
and another,
and another.

Here is Universal,
where Nagham the waitress knows
we have lots of lemon in our lentil soup,
lots of cigarettes in our pockets,
tells us to smile smile smile,
"because smiling is such, such, a nice thing to do."
The black kohl on her eyes is thicker
than memories and Turkish coffee,
darker than
the street outside.

Here we are,
drinking sunset and soup again,
watching time flutter
its paper wings,
weightless like a day in Hamra.
Here's to another day in Hamra,
and another,
and another.

Fresco

The coffee man carries the copper kettles on his back,
the sweet, the medium-sweet, the bitter,
claps the cups in the curves of his palms:
tik, titik, tsik, titik.

A breeze awakens, yawns, echoes
faintly, sleeps inside the afternoon;
our neighbor has a hard time
hanging her blankets,
tik, titik, tsik, titik, tik . . . there it goes.

The yellow porous building outside
has seen time with his cigar smoke,
seen time with his exaggerated legs—
time that sits. Still sits. Sits still
in his mediocre couch.

The twins play on the roof:
they spit on the people in the street
as their mother, waiting for her husband
to return from a Syrian prison,
yells at them from her chair,
stuffs and rolls our grape leaves,
the ones my mom will cook all night
on a small fire, with meat and bones.

The pushcart man shouts,
"Potatoes!"
I read some Verlaine,
light and inhale my boredom,
fail to turn it into ash,
"Potatoes!"
I shake my foot and the man still
screams for his living through the speaker,
"Potatoes!"
Les sanglots longs
Des violons

De l'automne
Blessent mon coeur
D'une langueur
Monotone.
"Potatoes!"

I watch the lightbulb cough
once, twice, once more,
and the lights are off.
"Watermelons!"
The truck driver arrives and drags along
his usual long, long, nasal voice
and the promise that his knife
will reveal the red, succulent heart.

Humidity is pure heaviness today.
The yellow building has lost its teeth,
and I wonder whether the red heart of a—
humidity is heavy today!—
whether the red heart of a watermelon
could cut through the heat.

The small fan stops.
I step out and watch
the steady August sky,
I dream of autumn and how
I'd like to water the clouds
so that rain would drop,
would drum a beat through my ennui,
tik, titik, tsik, titik.

The City Melts

when it rains
moonlight falls
thicker

when it rains
thicker and you can hear it
dripping from the rooftops

when it rains
faces flicker
in the shop windows

when it rains
the cars stop
their wave-like song

when it rains
they wade through the flooded streets
like islands moved by longing

when it rains
the heart is soaked
like a sock on a balcony

when it rains
you wonder whether the rain
is young or whether it's old

when it rains
the city melts
into the scent of the earth after rain.

Winged Carrots

You call them guardians,
these winged carrots
graffitied on the walls,
because you know
they take flight in your sleep,
land on rooftops, on clotheslines,
shield orphaned dreams
with their little black wings.

You call it *the sign*
because you have to look up
toward the sky to notice
it says "Rooms for Rent,"
it is white, it rusts
from an old balcony,
the Arabic letters flake.

You call him Thyme
because he sweeps his bakery,
gathers the day, the *zaatar* dust,
always at the same hour.
"*Bonjour*," he chants,
no matter what the time is,
as if words could lift
the falling darkness.

You call it orange,
this elevator with painted walls,
because in a city where walls
yield, where rails rust,
where litter fills the streets
like abandoned punctuation,
it has managed to keep
its color.

You call it god, this sidewalk,
because you carry it with you everywhere:
in your pockets, your footsteps.
You've memorized its bends like a prayer,
its long silver-gray hair,
its cigarettes, its favorite
songs and curse words,
the holes in its shirts.

You call it evening
because of the way the rain
seeps through the streetlights,
carries some of their radiance, drips
on the green garbage bags,
on the bottles your neighbor lines outside.

You call it Beirut
because you have no other name
for the way trees and antennas tilt in the wind,
the wind always, the certainty of the wind.

The Old Stairs of Beirut

They are definitely female.
I imagine them as an old woman
with fat knees, faint tattoos,
and the smell of piss.
I imagine them
as an old woman not afraid

of the love letters written
across her skin,
of baring her breasts
to the night sky.

They do not mock the world
for not knowing it is round,
for not knowing it turns
around itself,
for being fickle and so young,

and even in their old age,
even though they know
they are the opposite of walls,
they forgive.

They conspire only with the city,
for only the city understands
pale graffiti and chipped stone,
only the city understands
their descent into its heart,
only the city understands
not being tired of being

an immortal old woman
resting between garbage and art,
in the sun-punctured shade
that is almost a night sky
perforated with stars.

The City and the Sea

I cannot imagine a city
without a sea.

I cannot imagine a city without
windows that echo stories
like seashells. I can imagine
a city without clocks.

I cannot imagine a city
without a language that breaks
on the streets,
like the waves against the sand.
I can imagine
a city without statues.

I cannot imagine a city without
memories that flicker in the starlight
like sea salt. I can imagine
a city without traffic lights.

I cannot imagine a city without dance
planted in its soul
like a huge rock
in the Mediterranean sea.
I can imagine a city
without skyscrapers.

But not without a sky
invented by the sea.
Not without a sea.

The Shoe Store

We made jokes about that old
Hamra store, its unchanging
shoes, its smudged prices,
until our jokes thinned down
to a line we wore out
like a favorite shoe.

I try to recall
the you and me that I know
still exist somewhere on this street.
I look at my sepia fingers,
my hands, the sidewalk,
I recognize nothing

until I see the shoe store,
its eternal window
spitting in the face of time,
and I tell the shoes a joke I told
ten years ago,

watch the city unfold
its colors again,
like a woman with a peg in her mouth
standing behind a loaded clothesline.

II. Portrait of a Woman with a Cigarette

Service

Here in Beirut,
you do not stop
a cab. It stops
you.

Money is negotiable. Silence
isn't; small confidences in car mirrors,
    A woman cried all the way to work today
you have to have time for that.
Conversations seep
through the heat, the rain,
    That much for cucumbers!
hands instead of signal lights,
cigarette butts and

spit.
It takes time, it takes time
to master a driver's technique:
you have to gather it
in your throat like rage,
    Move! Move!
spit it out like
nothing, make it as ordinary
as a lemon on a table.

The car is the streets' old mistress.
It trembles, it swerves,
it dies little deaths along the way,
as the man behind the wheel adjusts
the word Allah or the cross
hanging from the rearview mirror,
    This country has no God, I tell you.
tilts his head toward
the sky inside the puddles,
toward a girl in tight jeans,
offers you a *zaatar manoushé*, insists,
tells you to forget
air conditioning.

Ali

He wasn't a beggar,
just someone who asked
for a smoke and talked to himself.
His right hand traced sentences
into broken circles
near his tilted head,
his eyes had seen
beyond language, couldn't find
their way back. His cigarette,

always hanging at a certain
angle between his lips,
almost parallel to his nose,
was his only anchor to the real world.

The people at West House
would sometimes give him a free haircut.
No one knew where he slept.
I think we believed he didn't,
that he just ceased to exist
beyond the corner.

We never saw him seated,
just a familiar pedestrian
who roamed the same
side of the street every day,
as if the distance
between Abu Naji and Universal were
the whole Mediterranean sea.
He walked and walked yet stayed
in place. Or maybe he didn't.

One day he pointed to a car,
said it was a Russian tank, named
the year it was manufactured.
Sometimes he gave random lectures
about communism.
We said hello or we didn't,
he replied or he didn't.

There were rumors
he was a professor gone mad,
that his whole family was killed
before him during the war,
but no one really knew anything
for sure about him, except that he was
as much a part of Bliss Street
as the students, the sidewalk, the fast food,
that he was one of the possible
definitions of the city.

Sonnet for Ali

For homeless Ali, who died of the cold

The first thing I'll do when I go back
to Bliss Street is imagine the way you turn
a corner. I'll buy coffee and a Marlboro pack,
walk among students who'd only learn

about you from a story growing old,
who don't see you there, like a god who's lost
track of the days and the word for *cold*.
I will lose you in the afternoon dust

of that shop that handed you coffee for free,
find you, then lose you again like a verse line,
a trench coat, follow you like a memory,
a ghost without a lighter, not that man who'd die

in the rain. Forgive me. I'll talk to myself too,
and place a cigarette where they found you.

Song of the Cat Woman

I've never planned on becoming this
woman calling out *beess, beess, beess*
on the stairs at night
with a broken voice, a glass in my hand.
But I got used to him lying on my doormat
like a dark pond, an omen, a reminder.

Once I knew about the sun, spilled
as if by accident, over the pavement;
I wore a red bikini and was someone's
lover. But even rooftops shift
their song in the dark.

Afif

There was a song about your name, Afif,
something about life being clean
like a street at dawn, something

about the days being evident and white
like an egg, the egg proud
like your name,

the song, of course, not taking itself
seriously, as we never took you seriously,
you the concierge with a limp and a nod.

It's not that you were memorable,
but you had the quality of eternal details,
like faded graffiti, abandoned newspapers,

or a few smudged notes, almost an offbeat
line, scribbled as if by mistake
amid the frenzy of Bliss Street.

Portrait of a Woman with a Cigarette

The world slants a little today—
the newspaper headlines,
the buildings, the borders, even
the sea line she's looking at.
She can almost see it
trying to lift its left shoulder,
trying to tip over its pain.

She moves her arm back and forth
to loosen this hurt,
familiar like a war wound
softened down to a whisper.
She knows how ache begets ache,
the way a pomegranate tree
can grow out of a cutting.

She listens to the traffic, crosses
her legs, lights a cigarette, tries
to forget the rust in her shoulder,
take in only the diagonal sea
and the sound of the coming rain.

Prayer

She climbed the university stairs
as if each step were a one-syllable
word worth lingering on.

When a cool breeze lifted
the leaves, she inhaled a brief
prayer of a breath, hid
in the purple jacaranda shade.

With one crisp circular move
she removed her blue veil,
placed it on her mouth as if
to soak up the colors on her lips,
watched daisies, carnations, almond flowers
blossom on its fabric,
wrapped it around her neck,

whipped the air with her long brown hair
whipped the air with her long brown hair
whipped the air with her long brown hair

to lash the spring sun rays,
the voices; to shed the veils
under the veil. She summoned God
by his ninety-nine names, walked
a little faster up the stairs,
as if she had existed in a different
morning, under a different
sky.

Souad

1. Water

My neighbor watched TV with her granddaughter
in the afternoons, wore stockings
that rolled down at the knees like a question
that keeps repeating itself.

She arranged her pots
like small silver elephants
on the cracked wooden shelves that still
carried the impossible weight.

Her husband faced the days
with a watering can.
His twig-like silhouette
rustled through the leaves
on the narrow kitchen balcony.

They rarely went to their quiet
house in the mountains.
She cooked, fed a two-year-old girl.
He disappeared, molded
a model of the garden he hoped
to have in heaven,
here on the first floor,
among the car honks.

2. Bread

I had forgotten to buy bread.
Walking under the rain, the hard rain,
there were other things to remember.
I decided to ask my neighbors
for a loaf or two, rehearsed my lines,
"I'm sorry . . ."

But she smiled, shook her head,
pulled me into the corridor,
thanked me for coming,
seated me on the burgundy sofa,
said she was doing okay
when little Farah was around,
but sometimes missed him
and held on tight until
the painful moment passed.

She said her name was Souad,
how nice it was of me,
a young student
from the university across the street,
I must have seen the death
notice on the wall, right?

Yes, yes, I apologized
for my pink shirt,
remembered out loud
that he used to water the plants.
She said she knew nothing
about plants, that they were dying,
that she hoped the rain would save
something.

3. Rain

Gunshots—
in the distance, then closer.
Perhaps another
assassination.
2005—a year
heavy, silent
with bombings.
I leapt

found my fists
banging at her door,
"Souad! Souad!"
heard footsteps,
glass breaking, keys.

"Firecrackers," she said.
"Probably a wedding."
I couldn't be sure
from my side of the building,
so she led me to her balcony,
her firm fingers on my arm as if
to root me back
in the muddy ground of real time.
She told me she knocked over
an old 7UP bottle
she used for olive oil.
We stood in our darkness,
watched the sky wounded
with colors
exploding, then falling
with a sound of rain,
a dark pond of olive oil
on the kitchen floor.

Nocturne

1.

The sky is a portrait of silence—
I could almost topple it,
watch the stars spill
out of its frame like dust.

The breeze ripples on the white sheet
falling from the clothesline
like a day washed, unwritten.

The cold ground is
waiting, waiting, waiting,
like water,
for a voice that does not come.

The streetlights quiver,
now yellow, now blue,
the moths do the dance that they do,
the red alarm in the car
counts one-two, one-two,
and the empty plastic chair
seems composed and tall.

2.

I watch silent
window-lights in the distance,
and a father twirling a cigarette in the air
to amuse his little girl.
I have an urge to say,
La ville est un lever de soleil nocturne,
the city is a nocturnal sunrise.

The woman in the window
kneels and prays,
songs and shisha smoke hover
over the distant café,

the tongues ululate in the bride's house,
the feet stamp, the palms play
a rhythmic Arabic beat,
Lilililililili!

3.

A drop of water breaks
against the ground,
as if time were leaking
from a balcony, turning
into a dark puddle
on this unreal street.

A stray dog measures
the day's remnants on the road,
a beggar snorts and spits,

the two old women on the first floor,
somebody's aunts,
place their shawls on their shoulders,
their wigs on the table,
move their rocking chairs—
the sound of the rocking wood
falls and rises
from the bottom of their souls.

4.

Allahu Akbar echoes—a distant cry
coming toward me from the moon
hanging by a thread in a sky
that begins to melt
under the faint flames of dawn.
I lift my empty glass, fill it
with the silky night,
drink it like black milk,
lick the dark that lingers on my lips.

III.
The Language
of *Salaam*

Parting with *La Figlia Che Piange*

"One day we will meet in New York,"
you said,
standing on the highest balcony.

"One day we will meet in New York,"
you said,
leaning on the rusty rails of dawn,
four in the morning receding into five.

"One day we will meet in New York,"
you said,
clasped your shawl to you inside
the autumness of Beirut,
the most, most autumn city night.

"One day we will meet in New York,"
you said,
the wind made you close your eyes and
turn, as I realized
I was parting with *La Figlia Che Piange,*
had an urge to tell you as you left,

"Stand on the highest Beirut balcony—
lean on the rusty rails—
weave, weave the moment in your hair—
clasp your shawl to you, close your tired eyes—
feel the autumn wind and turn
your back on the roofs and familiar skies:
but weave, weave the moment in your hair."

The Language of *Salaam*

Her English emails from the States
began with *Marhaba*, ended with
Salaam. She believed *Salaam*
declared itself, imposed
meaning. She said,

"In our language,
we repeat and repeat,
we call to the eye and the night,
we have so many absurdities
and words for love,
we have nuance, nuance,"
and "nuance," of course,
was her favorite word
in English and French.

"In our language," she said,
sketching her thoughts across the air,
"we have letters
that get stuck in your throat,
actual letters
that pronounce you.
And how could anyone not love Umm Kulthum?"

She counted in French, wrote in English,
was nostalgic, like us,
this Lycée, this American-University
generation, for Arabic,
and when she spoke the language of
Salaam, words melted in her mouth
like the setting sun.

Firecrackers

We were eating Tacos at Mark's place
when we heard it.
We held our fear in our fists,
tried to push it back into our veins,
ran to the balcony,
listened to the "Fire, fire,
firecrackers! Thank God, thank God,"
we licked the wine off our fingers
and decided to play cards.

Dana, she said,
tossing the queen of spades on the floor,
"We crazy children of the '80s, crazy
children of the war,"
and I wondered, *Is that what we are?*
Somehow the first things I saw
when I imagined that decade,

were Madonna, big hair, shoulder pads, glitter,
and a gray-and-black dress
that Mom wore for a dinner
where everyone took turns singing
Arabic songs, one of them
with a famous English line
that made everyone clap:
Do you love me, do you, do you?

Shelters, snipers, running down stairs
came later, perhaps at the same time, sometimes
never. How strange
that there was always a place
for the ordinary,
a place for two additional syllables
to fire—firecrackers.

I was smiling at my winning cards,
most of them hearts, when I told her
We crazy children of the war
reminded me of that teacher
who couldn't cross the street alone,
who wouldn't stir her coffee
in front of us, it was "too public,"
how she kept asking for the time,
how her long black hair seemed merely
an extension of her loneliness,
how we tried to understand
but in the end, she talked too much
and we were bored with nodding,
staring at our bare wrists.

The Old Building

Floor I

Water could not reach higher
than the first floor those days,
(that is what I recall)
so we spent our mornings going up
and down, up and down
to the first floor,
with buckets in our hands.
Mama sometimes sang and said
she had a great voice
and could've been a star.
I climbed and thought her voice
lifted the heat for a while,
resembled the water in our hands,
reflected the color of her eyes—
blue, inevitable, clear,
as I plunged into it and sang.
The stairs were more crowded
than the streets,
as if life were transferred
to that vertical world with yellow walls,
and permeated the small bullet holes.

Floor IV

I don't remember anyone's
name, except for the oldest son, Yasseen,
whose madness imposed itself on us,
whom we found from time to time,
unconscious on the night stairs,
like a garbage bag at our feet.

Floor V

Umm Jamal's laughter trembled,
settled in the fat around her waist.

As I ate she insisted
that I eat everything with bread,
told me her granddaughter
loved ketchup too.

One day she dusted her photo frames,
arranged them in sunlit angles,
braided her long winter hair in a bun,
pinned it to the back of her head
and stopped aging.

Floor VII

Raymond lived with his mother,
who went sideways down the stairs,
click, click, slowly, click,
(they say the war disturbs your walk).
Sometimes he sang in the shower
"Hiroshima, Hiroshima,
boom boom boom,
boom boom boom,"
until the ambulance flickered in the dark
like an ominous red star.

One day on the stairs,
time decided to
stop, cut itself in two,
let Raymond descend
from his room on the seventh.
I looked and told myself,
"Do not fear poor Raymond,
poor Raymond, he's so calm."

Floor IX

Ammo Jawad couldn't part
with the city, and its cafés, its streets.
On nights when the heat

grabbed you by the throat,
he slept on the balcony, smoked cigars,
wrote to his family in Dallas,
scribbled Arabic poetry across the sky
and dreamt
of the '60s, of fields of wild thyme
and a cold, light breeze.

Floor VI

The beautiful mother with blue eyes
shouted to the grocery store
from the balcony every other day,
I can still hear her say,
"Tomatoes, rice, tissues, and
Always, Always,
the thin ones please."
The father smoked Gitanes and
politics, wanted to change his car,
wanted to change his life.
He sang me to sleep every night,
planted my name
among olives and jasmine trees.
The little girl with crooked teeth
biked on the balcony with her brother,
remembers nothing of the civil war,
except a man singing to Hiroshima,
buckets filled with water, stairs,
and a little candle in the corridor
lit so she won't be afraid of the dark.

I Call It Home

This place where
electricity and water
take turns,
I call it home.

This place where
earth matters,
where we're dust and sand,
slip right through
the enemy's hands,
I call it home.

This place where
we die and rise
die and rise
again
every few years,
where we fold and
unfold peace
like a paper boat
(and hope it floats),
I call it home.

What the Revolution Taught Me
For Egypt, 2011

That death is
possible,
that words can

stampede like elephants
who walk in thousands
toward the water.

That your tongue is not
made of iron or lead,
that you could drop

this silence you hold
like a tray of steaming cups,
drop it, try,

and you will realize
that it burns
like a bomb in your hand,

that the fall
is not as long as you thought it was,
that the earth is closer

than you think.
That the world is still
conquerable,

that this is only possible
without blood and with
blood.

That blood is red,
like you expected,
and that it scares you.

That fear upon fear upon fear
upon fear upon fear finally
makes courage.

Egypt, Later
For Egypt, 2011

This is the moment when
later is irrelevant. Forget
later. Unlearn the false
linearity of time. Unlearn
the way you learn to learn lessons.

This is the moment.
Inhale it, for you are lucky
to have witnessed this—
what doesn't happen every day,
not even every century.

The opposite
happens every day,
and that is why we learn
words come out of eyelids,
metaphor is a survival skill.

Why again are you thinking of later?

*   *   *

Feel it,
for you have witnessed immortality
being born, not folding
her long gray hair.

Feel it,
for now you know
joy and sadness
have the same hands.

Feel it enough to plant it
among traumas, childhood memories, mothers,
all the songs you can't forget.

Feel it,
and if you do,
tear down this page and go
out on the streets.

Falling

You waved, jumped into
the water, you said two towers
in New York had
fallen. You smiled the way I did
when I heard of my grandfather's
death; we were too young.
A woman covered her legs
with almond oil, someone coughed,
the sun filtered
through the September clouds.

Our friend said Americans never die
like us. Why should we suffer
alone? He splashed seawater
on my face, dared me
to race him to the shore.
My eyes burnt. I'd heard
seawater resembled
amniotic fluid.

My mom kept yelling,
"Imagine yourself, your son,
having to jump
like that. Is violence ever—"
But he was too far,
his head half-immersed,
his arms beating
at the surface,
winning the race and I
floating on my back,
your palms in my hair,
my eyes shut, my arms full
of sea and sky,
open.

We were too young.
But somehow when the towers fell,

we felt the day shift,
felt the earth grow old—
a land of barbed wire
instead of rivers.
They're still falling now
in cities, in villages, in occupied lands,
people are still leaping
into the emptiness,
some dreaming of blood,
some dreaming of wings.

Correcting My Mother's Essay

My mother started writing essays
in English, essays with
wrong punctuation, wrong tenses,
wrong spacing, wrong spelling,
with Arabic
terms too, typed in English
(and a French accent)
when she cannot find
the translation for . . . *mina.*
In her email she tells me

she's very "exited" about this—
her American teacher loves her ideas,
even in her bad English.
Their topic this week is "Now and Then."
The teacher's given them two words:
"Boston   Marathon,"   asked
what it reminded them of.
My mom begins her essay by imagining

"the people who was about   to maratone,"
"how sad it is to be about to be running to your dying."
"Maybe they buy a new shoes yesterday," she writes,
"maybe they buy a new shoes for the maratone."
How sad, she knows, she knows how it feels like
"after you hear an explode,"
run to the phone
to check on your mother, your brother, your wife.

"Bad memories sleep," she writes, "but all of a suddenly,
all of a suddenly   they awake."
She remembers it now   that Friday.
How she walked to the pediatrician's
swinging me, three months old, from a basket
in her hand, my brother, five,
walking beside her.
She remembers his navy-blue clothes, his smile,

how the wind
"was taking his *blonde* hair straight aback."
She remembers the "suddenly explodes," the
"suddenly explodes,"
people running, cursing this country.
She remembers hiding
him in her jacket. "I couldn't breath,"
she writes, "I couldn't breath."
She remembers asking God
"to send all his angles! all his angles!"
to help her reach the building. She remembers
reaching the building in what felt
"like a worst century,"
finishing her own
"maratone."

She remembers watching
her "children   sleep   that night,"
"the night sky red, intense, explosions."
She remembers broken homes in her broken
English. "My hurt breaks today too," she writes,
"no matter where the killing is, my hurt breaks too."
She writes it all in her broken English that I dare not

correct. Nothing is wrong with your broken English,
Mom, nothing is wrong with your "Thanks God"
or the way you misspell "fiever" and "contry,"
the way you write "maingate"
instead of door. Nothing is wrong
mama, nothing, *mashi,*
with the way you "right"
"*Allah ynajjina*" instead of "God save us,"
you do not need to translate,
for we get it, *Mama,* we get it
in every broken   language,
with every broken   heart.

We Who Have Decided to Live in Autumn
Beirut, September 2012

The city's raging reds, her bellowing yellows,
her greens, her oranges,
are not autumn leaves,
for they don't know the art
of falling.
She abandons these poster colors
peeling from her body
(only to be glued again),
she abandons them to nuance,
to a hint of melancholy on the top of hats.

She takes off her shoes,
her flip-flops her nightclub high heels her army boots,
tosses them into the Mediterranean.
She lets her hair down,
long and loose upon her shoulders,
ready to resist.

> We've been cold in the summer
> with fear at the back of our necks,
> we lay with blankets over our heads
> instead of sleeping half-naked
> on balconies.
> We've burnt in winters,
> listened to the shooting
> of words, such empty bullets,
> learned to stand
> next to open refrigerator doors
> to keep our hearts from melting.
> We've known
> springs springing
> with cotton-candy hope,
> with promises of pink gazelles
> in the fields.

The city too has learned.
She knows
how to shed some bricks without breaking,
she hums
September, September,
all year,
to the fluttering sandwich papers on the streets,
lulls them, lures them,
into this wandering, this readiness
to lift and sink, to lift and sink again.

>   We don't know which fickle gods
>   control the chronology of our seasons,
>   but we've decided to live
>   in this permanent autumn
>   that offers no flowers,
>   yet leaves space enough
>   for the breeze.

>   We don't know when it began,
>   nor when it will end,
>   this un-season we've learned to savor,
>   this infinite in-betweeness.
>   We look at the sea. We imagine
>   seaweed sprouting out
>   of drowned shoes,
>   taking in the sunlight.

Peace: A Definition

One must imagine
a girl dancing somewhere
with a flag in her hands.

Imagine her on a hill against
a purple sky that's darkening
like an eggplant. Imagine her on a roof
among antennas or clotheslines,
her hair a white sheet.
Imagine her in the middle of the street,
standing on a red car, her arms
full of star and street light. Imagine her
dancing on that line where the sea
falls over, quivering like the question
mark or the small answer
in the middle of your heart.

One must imagine
a girl dancing somewhere
with a flag in her hands.

The flag is both familiar
and strange. You might have
drawn it when you were a child,
for it seems to have melted out
of your fingertips.
You might have touched it in your sleep,
for it has the texture of dreams.
You might have hummed it
as you crossed the street,
for it seems to have come out
of your mouth like a breath,
it's warm like that music note
you balance on your tongue.

One must imagine
a girl dancing somewhere
with a flag in her hands.

You were telling yourself
the world can begin or end
its wars. You'd struggled long enough
with the definition of peace.
You were thinking about the words
that didn't come, you passed a tree
with long, green hair, tried
to envision it awake at dawn,
filled with all the open eyes
that had once looked upon it,
you changed the radio channel, stopped
at a red traffic light and saw

a girl dancing somewhere
with a flag in her hands.

IV.
Palimpsest City

The One Who Weaves the Cities

He leans in his tin throne,
the one who weaves the cities.
He knows how to choose fabrics,
unwind cocoons, decides
on cotton or silk rain.

He knows which cities
have to be handmade,
casts shadows, considers
windows, rooftops,
is careful not
to spill his coffee
over the sunsets.

But sometimes he upturns
his cup like a fortune-teller, waits,
looks inside it to find his pattern;
some cities can only be born
out of the scent of coffee,
their sun a white
thumbprint
at the bottom of a coffee cup,
their streets like the lines
traced by dregs as thick
as the memories, the prophecies
on our sipping lips.

Love Poem

1. Hiding

The city opened its black cape:
university corners, dark cars, nightclubs,
and one time, that empty ladies' room
in a restaurant I forget,

where I smuggled you in
like a forbidden drug,
rushed you out
as soon as some woman
finished buttoning
her daughter's pants.

Even in your dorm room,
I was always ready
to hide in your closet
should your friend,
whose parents knew our parents,
who talked too much,
appear. You were so careful
not to tarnish my reputation.

"What's a reputation?" I asked.
You knew I was serious,
I was bending the word in my head,
tossing it, breaking it to see
if it were hollow,
if it were made of glass.
You understood better

the way people talked
about girls who went out
with boys they couldn't marry.
How they expected
a girl to consider
at least a possible
relationship.
How ours wasn't.

Not with your mother
lighting a candle every Sunday
to save you from my spell.
Not with my brother
reminding me
there was only one
God.

We learned to disappear,
were never caught,
except once at 3:00 a.m.,
when the police stopped and found us
drinking coffee on the *corniche*.
That's what we always did
after love: drank coffee by the sea,
had a sudden craving for fries.

And today as I fed our daughters fries,
you leaned in and whispered
in my ear, you leaned in and I

was ten years younger,
smiling, hiding
in your closet.

2. 200010848

There was no curfew,
but we had to stop by the university gate,
recite our names and ID numbers
to the security guard,
sign, go down to our dorms.

So no matter how drunk
with love or vodka I was,
I learned to tame my heavy tongue and utter,
"200010848."

One night after clubbing,
we drove through the city and I

was aware of nothing but car lights
scattered across the night street.
I pointed, told you to look
at those crystal words left
unsaid, glimmering in the distance.
You smiled, touched my forehead.

When you saw the police you warned me
not to say anything, anything at all.
You knew my words could betray
my reputation in pieces on the floor
of my head, the wings of our silent longing
trapped in the car, beating against the panes.

I nodded, lifted my thumb.
As you slowed down,
I stretched myself across your lap,
pulled down the car window,
tilted my head heavy with song and shouted,
"2000-10-8-48!"
watched the numbers dance
on the officer's paper, louder
than the notes of a saxophone.

Until Dawn

Pacifico:
pools of candle light
on each table—
we dived.
I called it "Candle Cup,"
imagined it written
in a curved, romantic font,
hid it in my purple bag,
made my way
among the smoke.
"A souvenir," I told Rana;
such superfluous stealing.
On Va S'aimer was playing
in the background.

1975:
a war-parody pub,
war-inspired décor.
Ziad Rahbani songs,
bullet marks, caps, Guevara
beards and *dabkeh*.
Dancing among the barricades.
We couldn't hear
what we were screaming
as we passed the drinks.

Hole in the Wall:
bachelorette party,
us dressed in crazy
'80s style, looking almost
like prostitutes.
Male stripper so
not sexy,
phallic cake.
Music burst out
into the cold
every time the bar door opened,
as if it wanted to dance
on the pavement too.

*   *   *

Pavement:
the other children were still trying
to sell chewing gum, but he
had stopped.
I gave him money,
he tossed it on the sidewalk,
wiped his cheeks,
said "Here, take it all,"
reached into his pockets,
threw the day's earnings
on the street like bread
for birds. I tried

to convince him to hold on
to the notes, but he knew
there was nothing to hold on to.
Knew it more than I did.
I asked how old he was:
five.

In the car my friend
banged the word
"God! God! God!"
against the steering wheel,
until it broke
into infinite little pieces
that flickered on the seats.
The power went out,
the generators hummed.
Allahu Akbar
from a nearby mosque.
The night already withdrawing
into the candle cup on my lap.
The day bleeding into the sky.
Dawn.

Palimpsest City

1.

Rana couldn't stop
dancing like a duck in Buddha Bar,
laughing her high-pitched laugh.
Later at the airport she waved,
licked her alcohol tears and screamed,
"I want my children to be just like you!"

That is the only airport moment
that I ever want to remember.

2.

The pub was called "So
Far," the name made us laugh.
The music was so
old, as old as the stairs, and so
was the woman in her thirties on the bar.
She looked like she'd been holding

that drink, that moment, that little hope,
for years in her right hand.

3.

We didn't drink that night,
but we lay on our backs
in the middle of the street,
jumped up at the sound
of an approaching car.
It was another way of knowing

we don't get to be so
young so often, so memorable.

4.

The way he looked at her, that girl
with lush electric curls.
Her eyes: wide enough for his longing.
He stood with his *Black Label* by the bead curtain
like one standing in the rain, smiling
at the thought of her thighs. I could tell
she reminded him of someone,
real or imaginary, that he wanted to love.

5.

Huda ordered a chicken sandwich
though she was trying to be vegetarian.
She pointed to the photos on the walls,
all dated around 1970, black-and-white;
her father used to eat here too. We might

find him, if we looked close enough,
in the background, his hair turning gray.

6.

We lightened the dark heavy nights
with caffeine, saw that theater actor
in his usual chair—not quite handsome,
and yet. We picked up war leaflets flung
from the sky, scribbled fuchsia flowers
on them. Everyday nothing still

happened, as nothing will,
in this palimpsest city, if you let it.

The Cafés Remember You When You're Gone

They imagine your laughter
above the chairs, look
for a trace of your voice
under the ashtrays, on the stairs.
They envision you
with your head tilted like this,
on the third table from the
left. They remember
how you tied
your hair one Sunday,
walked with your hands inside
your red coat
toward something they forget.
They almost cry at the sight
of an empty cup
that *you* could have left were you there,
were you there they would've known
how thick your coffee was, have measured
your dreams in the flick
of your lighter, your eyes.
They call out to you,
but you've learned not to listen
to the sound of your footsteps
or the songs of sunrise,
you wake up, you wake up
with your ankles swollen
from the distance
you have not crossed.
They invent you,
replay your red hair like a parting
scene in their sleep, in their sleep
they've seen
you with a missing tooth,
or standing beside a pool
in an evening gown,
your back turned, your hair
now longer, and brown.

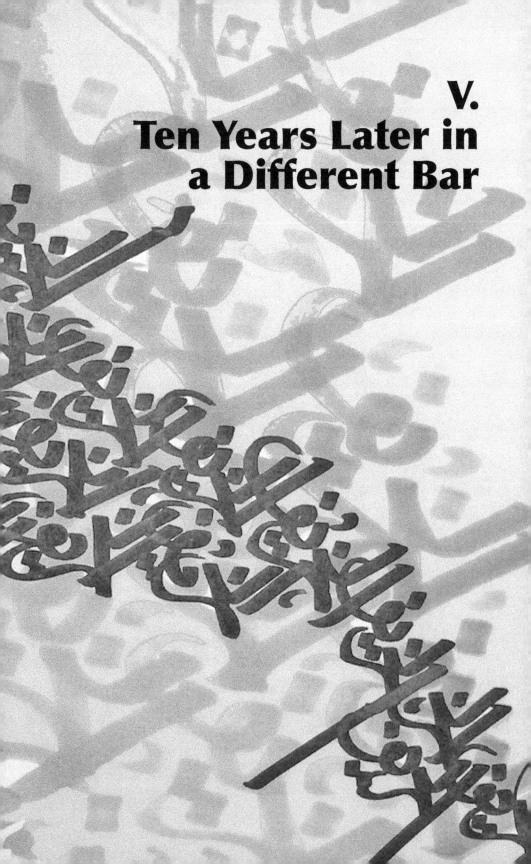

V.
Ten Years Later in a Different Bar

The Nameless

What do you call the space between
the written word and the blank page,
names in the distance and distance without names?

I know forgetting. I know
forgetting happens before
remembering.
But what happens after?

Give me a word
lukewarm and not so
comprehensible,
a word that drops
like white shadows
from the sky.

What name?
Give me a name
that melts like rain,
smells like moonlight
on my skin.

In Beirut

Like the meaning of poems,
they unfold inside my mind,
like rain they inspire me
to welcome the day,
it is them that wake me,
not the sun.
I didn't care much for the sun
when I had the streets of Beirut.

The balcony on the tenth floor
towers over the ugly roofs
(is there a tender word for *ugly?*),
and yet the moon steps down and chooses
to dance and flicker upon the roofs,
the gray moon-glazed roofs,
there are more roofs than buildings
as I look from the balcony
with autumn in my palms.
I didn't care much for beauty
when I had the balconies of Beirut.

Rain in Beirut is Beirut rain,
café lights glimmer in the rain,
how hypnotic they are,
like drowning yellow gods
who summon us for coffee,
how elastic time is and how irrelevant.
I didn't care much for the hours,
when I had the rain of Beirut.

Balcony

There is coffee, just enough
darkness, just enough lines
to reinvent. It's strong and the night
is stronger. It flows inside us,
inside the city,
and the city is stronger. There

is the city. It riddles
the dark with infinite
droplets of light.
Our fingers brush
the liquid threads it weaves.

We're on a balcony, the tenth
floor. From such height everything
seems small and all is larger.
From such height
one can begin
to understand, one can
be lost. From such height there is no
difference
between the weight that settles
and the one that
lifts.

Ten Years Later in a Different Bar

The city has changed like cities do;
the bar where we'd sing has closed.
We have changed like cities do.

There is an alley where the young, the new
drink their beer in sun-drenched clothes.
The city has changed likes cities do.

We once drank beers on the street too—
the bars too small for the dreams we chose.
We have changed like cities do.

Graffiti on the walls, red blazing blue,
says this city is more poetry than prose.
The city has changed like cities do.

Laure and I light up, smoke a few,
search for what we've dropped here: shadows.
We have changed like cities do.

The liquid light reminds me of you,
the laughter, the ceiling pipes—who knows
if the city has changed like cities do,
if we have changed like cities do.

The Lost City

I knew a city,
and I didn't need to summon it,
for it inhabited me.
This is where cities live,
inside the minds of people,
and this is where they begin
to die.

      Fling the day in anger, watch it,
      bounce off the walls,
      off their torn posters, graffiti, bullet holes.
      This is a place that knows
      how to rise, how to re-
      collect itself.

I knew the essence of the city I knew.
In it I felt space
had finally conquered time,

      Peel the moment bare
      like an orange, its scent,
      a fog in your palms

the corner of the street like a
corner of my mind—

      you had just sketched out
      in pencil the sound
      of those cars, those
      electric cables
      entwined across the sky

I knew the city's moves,
could shift her moods
better than the breeze and she

the imperfect circle
of that old man's
bicycle wheel,
the memories inside
that woman's walk.

would gather the moment
in the same way too,
say the same words
at the same time as we
both smiled.
And now when we meet,

        she recognizes you,
        (how could she forget?)
        tell yourself

It's probably
the heat, it must be
the heat that alienates,

        remind each other

not always of the same lines

        watch a girl run toward her lover

with *finally, finally*, in her steps, her eyes,

        lift her yellow shawl,   fling it,

like absence at our feet.

Bench

This is the bench we choose
because it has more shade, these
are the trees, this is the Mediterranean.
We sit here, we fix the sea
with our eyes and it does not
fight back, it is wide and clear enough
to embrace our talk our illusions.
We talk. We have young hands
we move them
because we believe
they matter. We read.
Mostly the day but also poetry
we find out it's better when it's spoken.
People pass by, look, but we
are not being theatrical just
true. I inhale a cigarette perhaps
for show but also for the light
bitterness.

This is the bench, it has a small
engraving, it says
someone relatively important
declared this the most beautiful
view in the Middle East. We laugh
at those Westerners romanticizing
our sea, and yet
we come back here every day
and yet we plan
to come back here when our hands
have bulging veins,
after all the distractions
of land in between.

Samaa'

We who were students then,
unstoppable, useless, bored, amused, bewildered,
taking to the streets together,
to coffee, to alcohol, to poetry,
becoming, becoming,
are now mothers,
in different continents, in countries
that are neither hell nor home.

You call, tell me you feel shell-shocked.
Your daughter is six months old,
you've called her *Samaa'*,
a name vast, strange,
yet almost at an arm's length
every time I look at the sky.

I am selfish, you say, *I am not
big on sacrifice.*
I tell you anyone who is
lacks purpose or attention,
you say *purpose AND attention*,
you laugh.
You don't tell me you want
to be held, but I take your hand

back to Beirut alleys where we follow
two girls in their twenties
who have our faces, our eyes,
and their eyes are as vast as *samaa'*
and I say, look,

our daughters have been there all along,
we have been there all along,
ever familiar, ever estranged.

Dance
Dubai, 2012

Here I am,
on a balcony in another city,
trying to summon, trying to mourn
a different city,
when stronger than the heat
rises music.
Someone must be having the same
party I was having
ten years ago, for I swear I hear
the same songs, so how
can I resist?

Alone and lonely
on a balcony I dance.
I dance I lift my arms I remember
dark clubs and hands,
I remember a red shirt that fell
perfect around my belly button, I remember being
(do I dare use the word?)
careless,
lightheaded in hallways beating
with music, I remember
going to my morning class half-drunk
yet still making sense,
what clarity, what utter uselessness,
I remember the nights beginning
at the start of the day, the day
tripping into itself at the end of a night,
I remember friends with nothing but words
and time, and time, and time,
talking to the city as if the city understood,
I move my waist, my neck, I sweat,

(where on earth is this music coming from?)
I re-member you Beirut,
the heat the traffic the craziness the cigarettes

the melting mascara the smeared rooftops
the garbage the godless god-full sky the rain,
and I dance as you explode again today
and I dance as I explode again today
(let it rain let it rain let it rain)
I dance on your balconies
here in this desert until
a faint female voice calls out
a question, says *turn*—

we carry cities, instead of angels,
on our shoulders, we trail them
behind us like old hurts.

Self-portrait on Bliss Street

I bought a Philly Steak:
the man leaning on his car
with a sandwich in his hand
said it was the most popular,
that the only way of eating it
was inside the noise of the street.

I tried to move as if
I knew exactly
who I was and where
I was going,
squeezing ketchup on the bread
before each bite.

It gave me nothing, this Beirut,
except an English song about pizza,
love, and the moon, spilling out
of the *manoush* oven on my left,
dancing toward me in Arabic.

I imagined what it would be like
to catch my name
tossed at me from a balcony,
or heaved by a boyfriend
from a moving car I'd just
stormed out of,

what it would be like years
later, when we sang *That's Amore*
to the red stop-sign on the corner,
the broken telephone booth,
the war-torn newspapers,
traced the street once, twice,
ten times an afternoon, a night, a dawn,
like idle children who are never bored
of little stories told and retold.

Ghazal: Dream-fig

Forgotten—how to deal with darkness, feel the walls in you,
drip candle wax for balance, find my breath within. You.

A little girl climbed the stairs two by two, reciting the neighbors'
door ornaments: horse-shoe, prayer, plant, wood, tin, you.

The grocer's fat name, the peanut-butter chips, the smell
of the street on the dusty shelves. The heat a skin: you.

My step-grandmother paid the butcher by tossing the money
from the fifth in a laundry pin. Balconies: where I would begin you.

Somewhere I'm still stuck in an elevator, banging on the door,
waiting to be lifted up, which is a kind of abandoning you.

My father, on the phone, justifies you, "Gunshots, yes, though nothing
unusual." To keep fear close enough, yet separate: a twin, you.

Even when I don't name you, you're in the middle, beginning,
end of all my sentences. You are my sentence, my writing jinn, you.

Last night I dreamt my fridge was full of figs. I peeled
the one bursting with blue-red. Lebanon, dream-fig, sin—you.

Rewriting Beyrouth

You read like the error
of a child who's just learnt
the magic, the possibility,
of combining letters.

To write you down
is like writing with rain, with thirst.
To spell you is always
a spell gone wrong,

a potion where one forgets,
or invents,
a thread of light, footsteps,
the scent of coffee.

Beyroot for the mud, the search,
the reaching out,
but also for the certainty
of the earth.

Byerouth for the Arabic
effect, the right pronunciation,
for the sound of distance
in the cold. *Byerouth*
for a transliteration on the walls
of a café *à la mode*.

Beyroute for streets
flickering backward
like memories into my head.

I prefer to keep
the *th* at the end,
absolute like a *the*,
hesitant like a lisp,
a small *h* masquerading as silence,
a journey interrupted or not knowing
how to end.

Spring

There are poverties and there are poverties.
— Adrienne Rich

I hear your neighbor has trouble sleeping, trouble eating,
that she changes her door locks every week and has brought
all her plants indoors, hid her Bible under the mattress.
Though the streets are not safe, you say, you still go out
every night to forget—or is it to remember? Am I exaggerating?

I hear Hamra is not the same anymore: Syrian
refugees on the streets, men begging, children selling
roses, selling roses, why are the doomed always selling roses?
You say you don't know whether to fear for them or fear them.

I hear these borders have been failing, have failed, will fail,
these fake borders will shift like continents, I wonder
whether memory could go back to the supercontinent, tell me
who is holding the big crayons this time, and what color
will our share of sky be, to which God will it be forced to answer?

There is exile, my friend, and there is exile.

My husband, he keeps telling me the *Salafis*
are coming, the *Salafis* are coming, says we
should sell the house and buy one here,
in this exile, this desert, because home
is no longer the home we knew when we were young,
and I shout, I laugh, I break something, tell him home was never
the home we knew, the one we wanted, the one
we imagined when we were young and didn't listen

to the evening news, heard only the absurd voices inside us,
those voices with big hands that pushed us fully clothed
off high rocks and into the icy water, our arms beating
like wings to fly back up from its dark depth for breath.

I tell him I believe, I still believe, I repeat myself
like that broken CD of ours that got stuck on "will always, will always,"
but he has burnt holy books, newspapers, manifestos, a long time ago,
like one who's lost in the woods and wants to scare away the wolves.
He wakes me up in the middle of the night, hand brushing my breast,
and tells me to look, listen to that Palestinian guy from Gaza,
he's the new Arab Idol, he used to sing at weddings,
never got paid, crossed borders, climbed walls, smuggled
his dream, just to feed a little prayer into this microphone.

There is religion, my friend, and there is religion.

You say the theaters are still open, and I see red wooden doors,
and people eager to watch that play enacted by the inmates
of that horrible prison, and that play by the patients in the psychiatric
ward, and that play about a woman who wakes her husband
in the early morning to tell him she might have stopped knowing
how to trace the aroma of her coffee back to their occupied house.

I hear we are still running marathons and exhaling shisha smoke,
I hear we're still diving in this polluted sea, diving in this polluted
sky, looking for our black hearts like precious pearls,
singing songs that are either about love or our country,
and better still, about love *and* our country, for we want them both
to open their arms and take us into their mud, their pain.

There is longing, my friend, and there is longing.

I tell you the shooting is heavier in Tripoli this Friday,
that people are afraid of prayer day now, they're afraid of prayer;
will the sound of the *azan* never be pure to my ears again? Listen,
the shooting is heavier in Tripoli today, so don't take that roundabout,
the one with the word *Allah* painted green, it's probably blocked,
all motorcycles and black smoke, tires burning, people cursing
around it in the name of this stone-God erected in its middle.

I gulped tequila shots and danced until dawn, until the phone
rang and I was told my daughter was feverish, no Panadol
would do, and I knew it was another kind of fever, the kind

that a child who longs for her mother burns with, the kind the exiled
longing for their houses burn with, the kind that could fill mountains
with hate like lava, turn them into volcanos, these mountains
that never wanted anything but a little sun, a little air, a little grass.

There is guilt, my friend, and there is guilt.

I hear your friend in Damascus who has three kids hasn't left,
crosses herself many times a day, convinces herself life is fine,
life is fine and doesn't care who wins, really, she just
wants her boys to play football in the street again.
I tell you, *See?* Egypt hasn't given up, I knew it wouldn't,
not Egypt, no, and of course I exaggerate but who cares
about the Second Coming now that we have a Second Revolution?
You say the word revolution also means turning around something else.
I ask you about that tree with beautiful leaves across the street, is it
still there? Does the wind still release the song of the sea from
its branches? You say it's strange that I only seem to remember it
in spring, you remind me that the leaves I listen to every year
are different leaves that have replaced the fallen ones,
that they have no memory of you and me on this street,

perhaps it's better to look for ourselves in the brown ones rustling
on the floor. You say we might be on the verge, on the verge
of another civil war, and what on earth do we do
if it comes, how long can one pretend to exist outside of this,
when blood might flood the streets instead of rain?
What flowers will grow then? And where will we bury our dead?

There is spring, my friend, and there is spring.

Notes

p. 4: Hamra is a famous street in Beirut. Modca is one of the oldest Beirut cafés, replaced in 2003 by a Vero Moda clothes shop.

p. 6: *ya leil ya ein* literally translates as "Oh night, oh eye," a common expression used in Arabic songs.

pp. 8–9: The French poetry is the first stanza of Verlaine's poem, "Chanson d'automne."

p. 14: The rock is an allusion to Raouché, a landmark consisting of two huge rock foundations in the sea of Beirut.

p. 19: In Lebanon, *service* is a French term used for "taxi." A *manoushé* is a Lebanese pastry similar to pizza.

p. 23: *Beess* means "cat" in Arabic.

p. 24: Afif is an Arabic name that means "chaste."

p. 35: The title of the poem takes after T. S. Eliot's "La Figlia Che Piange."

p. 36: In Arabic, *Salaam* means "peace" and *Marhaba* means "hello."

p. 40: *Ammo* is the Arabic term for uncle.

p. 41: "Always" is a brand of sanitary pads.

p. 47: *Mina* is Arabic for "port."

p. 74: *Samaa'* means "sky" in Arabic.

p. 79: "Beyrouth" is another spelling of Beirut.

Acknowledgments

Thanks to the editors of the journals/anthologies in which the following poems first appeared (sometimes in earlier versions):

Arabesques Review: "To Hamra"
The Common: "Parting with *La Figlia Che Piange*" and "Balcony"
Copper Nickel: "The Old Building"
Cream City Review: "What the Revolution Taught Me"
Crosstimbers: "The Old Stairs of Beirut," "In Beirut," and "The City and the Sea"
Folio: "Egypt, Later"
Mizna: "Fresco," "Afif," and "Firecrackers"
Nimrod: "Rewriting Beyrouth"
Ploughshares: "Correcting My Mother's Essay"
Poetry Northwest: "We Who Have Decided to Live in Autumn" and "Bench"
Quiddity: "Service" and "I Call It Home"
Sampsonia's Way: "The Lost City"
Silk Road: "The Nameless"
Spherical Tabby (web audio): "Spring"
Sukoon: "A Few Love Lines to Beirut," "The Language of *Salaam*," and "Spring"

"We Who Have Decided to Live in Autumn" and "Bench" are included in *The Columbia Granger's World of Poetry*; "Winged Carrots" is in *Not Somewhere Else But Here: A Contemporary Anthology of Women and Place* (Sundress Publications, 2014) and in *The Emma Press Anthology of Homesickness and Exile* (The Emma Press, 2014); "Ten Years Later in a Different Bar" is in *The Emma Press Anthology of Homesickness and Exile* (The Emma Press, 2014); "The Lost City" and "Palimpsest City" are included in *Nowhere Near a Damn Rainbow: Unsanctioned Writing from the Middle East* (xanadu, 2012).

Thank you, Mom, for turning to that little girl in the kitchen and telling her she was going to become a writer. Thank you to my husband and my *habibi*, Marwan El-Nakat, and my daughters, Leina and Aya, for your support and for all the love and joy you bring into my life every second. Thank you, Huda Fakhreddine, without whom Beirut would not have been the same. Thank you, Rana Kamareddine, a childhood friend who loved, listened, encouraged, and believed. A very special thanks to Irish poet Frank Dullaghan, an amazing friend and mentor, who has given me confidence and guidance and helped me polish this manuscript. Thank you to poet and editor Sarah Webb, who has encouraged me and given me input on my manuscript. I'm eternally grateful to judge and poet Lola Haskins for believing in my voice. Thank you to Greg Kosmicki, James Cihlar, Susan Ramundo, Chris Bristol, Aaron Anstett, and everyone at The Backwaters Press who worked on making this book happen. Thank you to my friends, who have dealt with my obsession and were there for me: Rania Turk, Lina Abyad, Nada Qaissi, Layla Ghandour, Laure Chedrawi, and Rami El-Nakat. A big thank you to my poet friends who supported, understood, and encouraged: Hind Shoufani (and her platform Poeticians), Rewa Zeinati, Danna Lorch, and Cath Mason. Thank you, Yazan Halwani, for the beautiful cover art.

Gratefulness for everything, or as we say in Arabic, *hamdillah*.

About the Author

Zeina Hashem Beck is a Lebanese poet with a BA and an MA in English Literature from the American University of Beirut. She's been nominated for a Pushcart Prize, and her poems have been published or are forthcoming in *Ploughshares*, *Nimrod*, *Poetry Northwest*, *The Common*, *Cream City Review*, *Quiddity*, *Copper Nickel*, *Mizna*, *The Midwest Quarterly*, and *Mslexia*, among others. Zeina is a strong performer of her work. She lives with her husband and two daughters in Dubai, where she runs poetry workshops, reads regularly, and hosts PUNCH, a Dubai-based poetry and open-mic collective. Her website is www.zeinahashembeck.com.

Lightning Source UK Ltd.
Milton Keynes UK
UKHW011356290421
382821UK00011B/351